Fire TV Users Manual

Bring Your Favorite Movies and TV Shows, Video Games and Apps to Your Living Room

By Steve Weber

Published by Stephen W. Weber
Weber Books www.WeberBooks.com
ISBN: 978-1-936560-21-9

Contents

Introduction

Unprecedented. Never has such a universe of entertainment and education been packed into such a small package. Amazon's Fire TV has three times the processing power and four times the memory of any competing home-electronics gadget. It's truly a premium product at a bargain price.

Fire TV brings a menu of more than 200,000 movies and TV episodes to your fingertips. It's a huge, open ecosystem of entertainment. Plus, it comes with access to the best video games.

The Fire TV, the little box that plugs into your HDTV, provides instant access to every leading video-streaming service—Netflix, Amazon Instant Video, Hulu Plus, WatchESPN, and Showtime. New movie releases are available for low-cost rentals. And the FireTV brings much more of your personal media to your TV—photos, home video, and music. You can play slide shows and find specific photos. Photos or videos you take on your phone or tablet can be uploaded to Amazon Cloud Drive and appear on your TV within seconds.

Here are the must-have features Fire TV delivers:

- **Voice search that just works**. It's perhaps the biggest leap forward with Fire TV. No more scrolling and pecking letters from an alphabet grid, you simply mention the name of a movie, TV show, actor, director or genre.
- **Every leading streaming-video service**. They're all available on your TV, plus a world of music—Amazon MP3s, Pandora, iHeartRadio, TuneIn and more. With X-Ray for Music, lyrics display and scroll line-by-line automatically as the song plays.
- **World-class performance in a tiny box**. It's a quad-core processor with more than three times the muscle of the competitors—Apple TV, Chromecast, or Roku 3. It's True HDTV plus Dolby Digital Plus surround sound.
- **Ready to use, right out of the box**. After you order your Fire TV from Amazon, the unit arrives pre-registered to your Amazon account. Just take it out of the box, plug it in, and start enjoying it.
- **Advanced Streaming and Prediction (ASAP).** This predicts which movies and shows you'll want to watch and pre-loads them for you.
- **High-quality gaming without the expense of a game console**. Enjoy games like Minecraft, Monsters University, The Game of Life, The Walking Dead, NBA2K14, Asphalt 8, and much more. The average prices of Fire TV games is a measly $1.85.
- **Revolutionary parental controls**. You can choose what your kids see and you can set time limits for the types of content and times of day. No more arguments at bedtime. FreeTime Unlimited provides an all-you-can-eat subscription for kids aged 3 to 8.

More than just a gadget, Fire TV is a seamlessly integrated service that manages your entertainment experience, including features like:

- **Whispersync**—Preserves and synchronizes your video and music library across all of your devices. You can start watching a movie on your Kindle Fire tablet, then switch to your living-room TV. The video resumes exactly where you left off. The same is true for games. You can switch devices seamlessly.

- **Worry-free archive**—Your digital content is automatically backed up to Amazon's cloud. No worries about losing your collection.
- **Great customer service**—With Amazon, help is just a phone call or email away. If you're using your Kindle Fire, you can tap the Mayday button for live assistance.
- **Free month of Amazon Prime and Netflix**—With your Fire TV purchase, you get free month-long trials of these compelling platforms. The Amazon Prime package includes exclusive movies, shows, books and reduced shipping fees for Amazon purchases. Netflix brings you instant access to a vast selection of movies and TV shows.

Okay, that's enough talk. Let's get started. But first, you will need an HDMI cable to connect the Fire's box to your TV. Just like that first printer you ever hooked up, you will need a cable that isn't included with the printer. If you don't have an HDMI cable, you will need to order one online or buy one from a store that sells electronics. Amazon sells one for about $6.

1 ► FAST START GUIDE

To get started, we've got three items on our agenda:

1. Connecting the Fire TV console.
2. Connecting the system to your home Internet network.
3. Registering your Fire TV (if necessary).

What's in the Box

Your Fire TV is delivered with these items:

- Amazon Fire TV console
- Remote control
- Two AAA batteries
- Power adapter

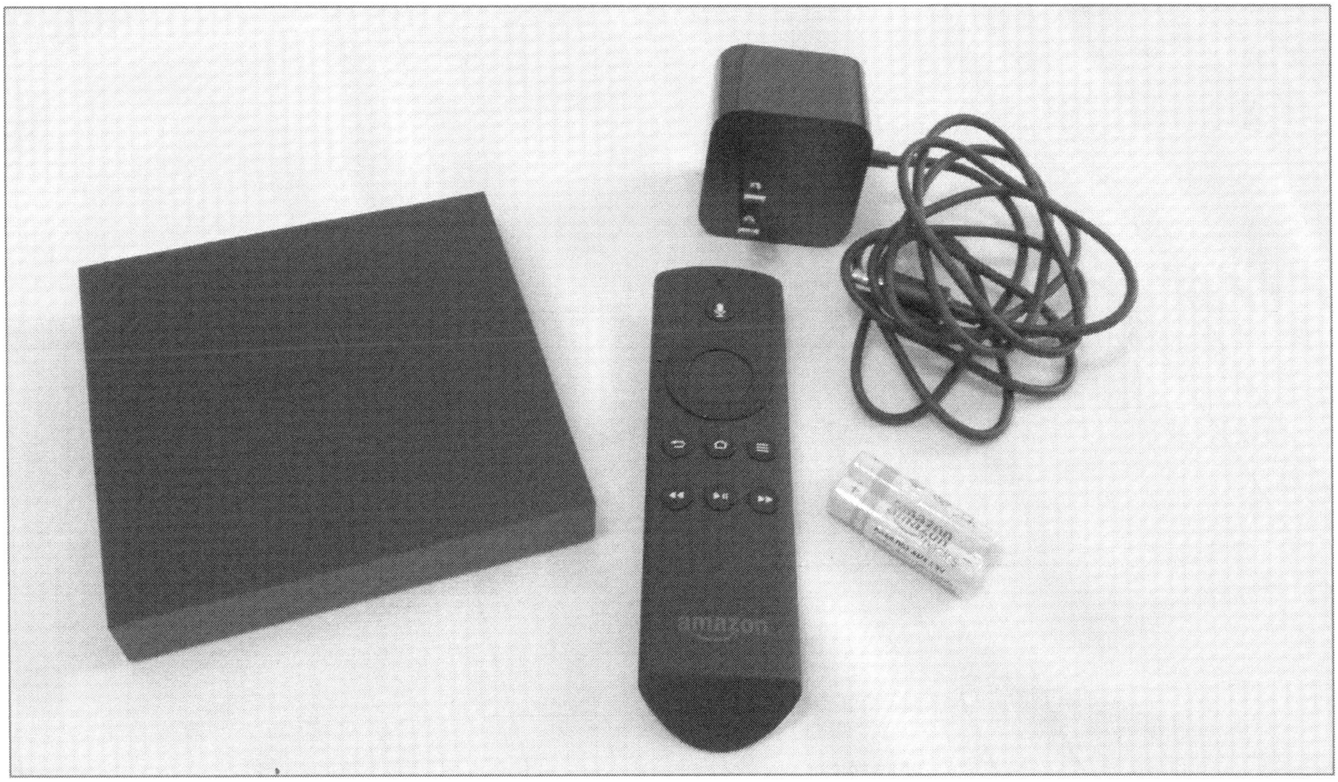

Let's take a closer look at the ports on the back of the Fire TV console:

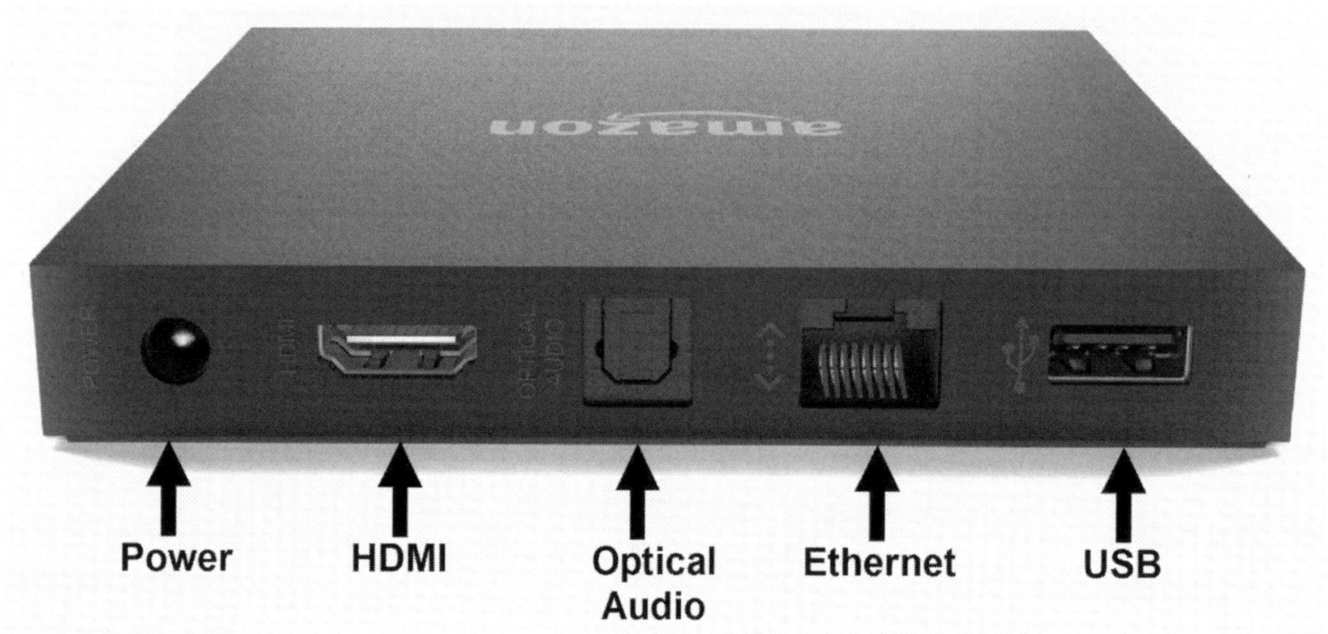

◎ **Power:** The Power port connects your console to a power outlet using the included power adapter. A blinking white light on the front of the console means your Fire TV is turning on or is searching for a remote control. (To turn off the Fire TV, you can unplug the power cord. However, it's not necessary to turn off the unit when you're finished using it—the console enters sleep mode after 30 minutes of non-use.)

HDMI: The HDMI port connects the console to your television. An HDMI cable isn't included in the box. These range in price from $5 to $30, depending on where you shop.

Optical audio: This port can be used to connect the console to a stereo. This is optional, and an optical cable isn't included in the box.

Ethernet: This port can be used to connect your console to a router or a modem. A wired connection isn't required and an ethernet cable isn't included in the box.

USB: The USB port doesn't yet support any accessories.

And let's take a closer look at the remote control:

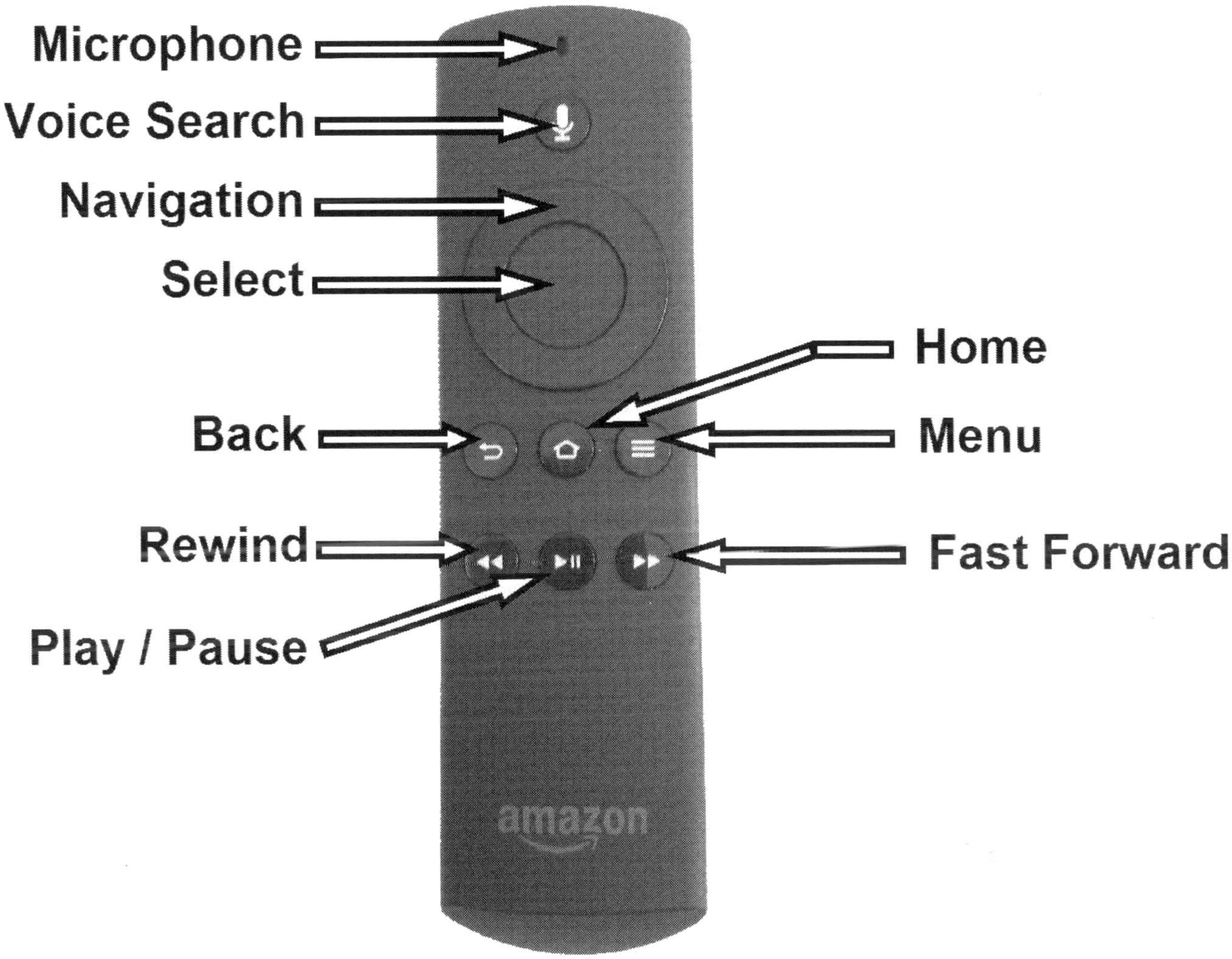

Connect Fire TV to Your Television

You'll need that HDMI cable to connect your Fire TV.

Connect one end of the HDMI cable into the HDMI port on the Amazon Fire TV console. Plug the other end of the cable into an HDMI port on your television. (If your TV is connected to an audio-video home-entertainment receiver, you should plug the HDMI cable into your receiver.)

1. Plug the power cable into the Fire TV console, then into a wall power outlet.
2. Turn on your TV and use your TV's remote to select the HDMI input your Fire TV is connected to.
3. Insert the batteries into your remote control. The remote should connect automatically. If not, verify that you've inserted the batteries in the correct orientation, then press the **Home** button for at least five seconds, then release it.
4. Don't enclose Fire TV in a cabinet as this may reduce signal strength.

Fire TV is now connected to your TV, and you'll see on-screen instructions to complete your setup.

Connect Fire TV to Your Home Internet Network

You can connect the Fire TV to your home network by using either of these methods:

Wi-Fi Network

1. Using the remote control, select your home network from the list displayed on the screen. If the name of your network isn't visible, enter your network's name.

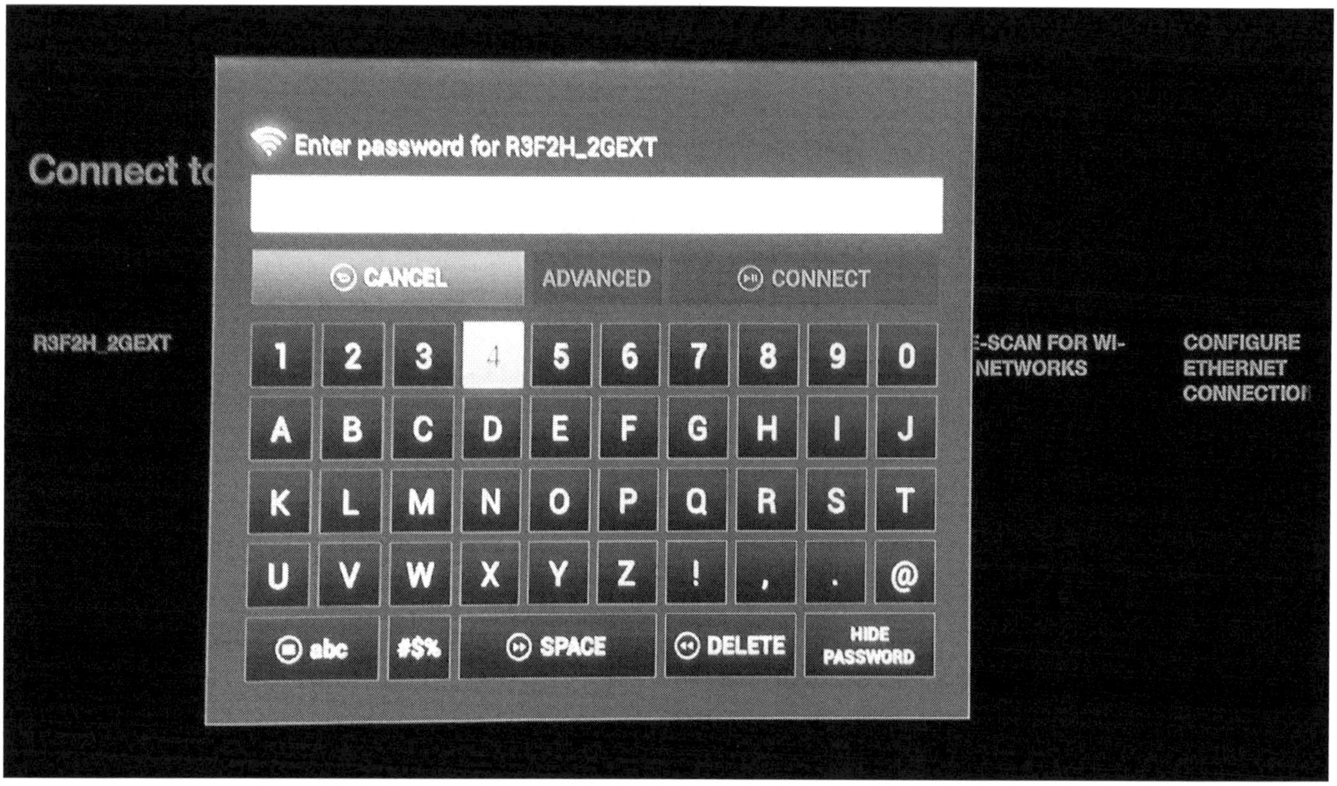

2. Enter your network's password, if necessary, using the on-screen keyboard.

—OR—

Wired Network

1. Connect one end of an ethernet cable (not included) to your router. Connect the other end to the back of your Fire TV console.
2. Fire TV will detect your network and continue the setup.

After your Fire TV console connects with your home network, your unit will download the most recent software updates. Depending on the speed of your Internet connection, this updating process will require about five to 10 minutes. Then the updates will install and your console will restart.

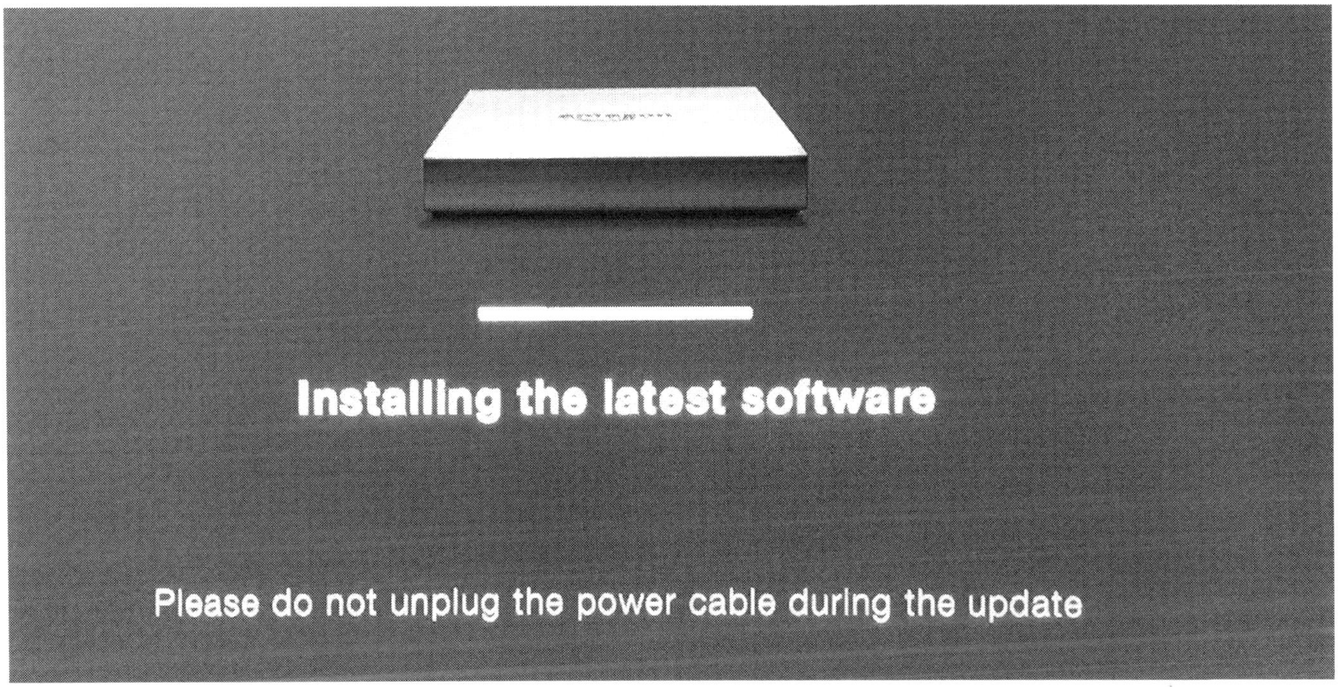

Registering Your Fire TV

If you purchased the Fire TV using your Amazon account, it's delivered already registered. If you received the unit as a gift or it's not yet registered, follow the on-screen instructions to register.

Getting Help from Amazon

For troubleshooting tips, visit www.amazon.com/firetvsupport

2 ▶ BASIC NAVIGATION AND ACCESSING CONTENT

Use the remote control to access your **Home** screen and your movies, TV shows, games and apps. The circular track pad enables you to move up, down, left or right. The middle of the track pad lets you **Select** a content item, function or category.

- To go to the **Home** screen, press the **Home** button
- To return to the previous screen, press the **Back** button
- To select a movie, TV show, game or app, press the **Select** button
- To wake up the Fire TV console, press any button. Your unit enters sleep mode after 30 minutes of no activity.

Navigate the Main Menu

The **Home** screen includes the **Main Menu**, which allows you to access your account and device settings, as well as movie, TV show, game, and app content libraries.

From any screen on Fire TV, press the **Home** button to return to the **Home** screen and **Main Menu** options. Here are the options at the **Main Menu**:

- **Search**: Search for movies, TV shows, games, apps and music videos from Vevo. Use the remote control to search for content titles using voice input or the onscreen keyboard.
- **Home**: Review content recommendations and recent activity.
    1. **Recent** – Your recently viewed movies, TV shows, games or apps. You can remove an item from **Recent** by navigating to the item and selecting **Remove from Recent**.
    2. **Featured Movies & TV** or **Apps & Games** – Special promotions featured by Amazon and other content providers. You can't remove items from the **Featured** listings.
    3. **Other Movies, TV, Apps & Games** – Includes categories like **New Releases**, **Recently Added to Prime**, **Top Movies**, **Free Games**, **Recommended Movies** and **Recommended TV**. You can only remove items from **Recommended Movies** and **TV** listings.

- **Movies**: Rent, buy and watch movies from the Amazon Instant Video store. If you're a Prime member, you can watch Prime Instant Video at no extra cost.
- **TV**: Buy and watch TV show episodes or seasons from the Amazon Instant Video store. If you're a Prime member, you can watch Prime videos at no extra cost.
- **Watchlist**: Access your Instant Video Watchlist, a list of movies or TV shows you've identified for watching later. Once you buy or rent the title, it's available for streaming from your Video Library.
- **Video Library**: Includes all the Instant Video movies and TV shows you've purchased or are currently renting, but doesn't include items you've watched through Prime Instant Video. Purchased content is stored in the Cloud and is available for streaming.

Note: Videos from third-party apps like Netflix and Hulu are reached directly from the apps, not from the Video Library.

- **Games**: Shop for, buy and play games from Amazon's Appstore. Use your GameCircle profile to view and compare scores, leaderboards, and time played in a game. You can pair Amazon Fire or Bluetooth game controllers with Amazon Fire TV.
- **Apps**: Shop for and buy games and apps from Amazon's Appstore.
- **Photos**: View photos and personal videos from your Amazon Cloud Drive account. You can start photo slideshows and designate certain photos as screen savers.
- **Settings**: View and manage your Amazon Fire TV apps, controllers, parental controls, Internet connection, and more.

Buy or Rent Movies and TV Shows

Using your Fire TV, you can buy, rent and watch Amazon Instant Video movies and TV shows. When you rent videos, you can watch them for a specified time period. When you purchase videos, they're accessible from **Your Video Library** and you can watch them as often as you wish.

1. Locate the movies you want to buy or rent:
   - Browse through the categories under **Movies** or **TV**.
   - From the **Home** screen, select **Search** to search for Amazon movies or TV shows. Press and hold the **Voice** button  on your remote to search using your voice or press up to use an on-screen keyboard.
2. From the search results, select a movie or TV show to view its product detail page.
3. Select **Buy** or **Rent** and follow the on-screen instructions. Your purchase is charged to your 1-Click payment method and stored in **Your Video Library**.

Movies and TV shows from third-party apps are only accessible through the apps, not **Your Video Library**.

Select **Add to Watchlist** to mark items you want to view later. Select **Watch Now** to immediately watch the video.

Use Your Voice to Search Amazon Fire TV

You can use your remote control for voice-initiated searching for movies, TV shows, apps, games and more. The voice search is a "keyboard replacement" and doesn't support "natural language" commands. That means you must confine your voice input to keywords like a movie title or actor's name, not use full sentences like "I feel like watching a scary movie."

1. On your Amazon Fire TV remote, press and hold the **Voice** button. A microphone icon should appear on the screen.
2. Holding the remote control a few inches away from your mouth, speak keywords related to the content you're searching for, then release the **Voice** button.
3. Fire TV searches your content library, the Amazon stores, and any compatible app for related content. Search results appear on your TV screen.

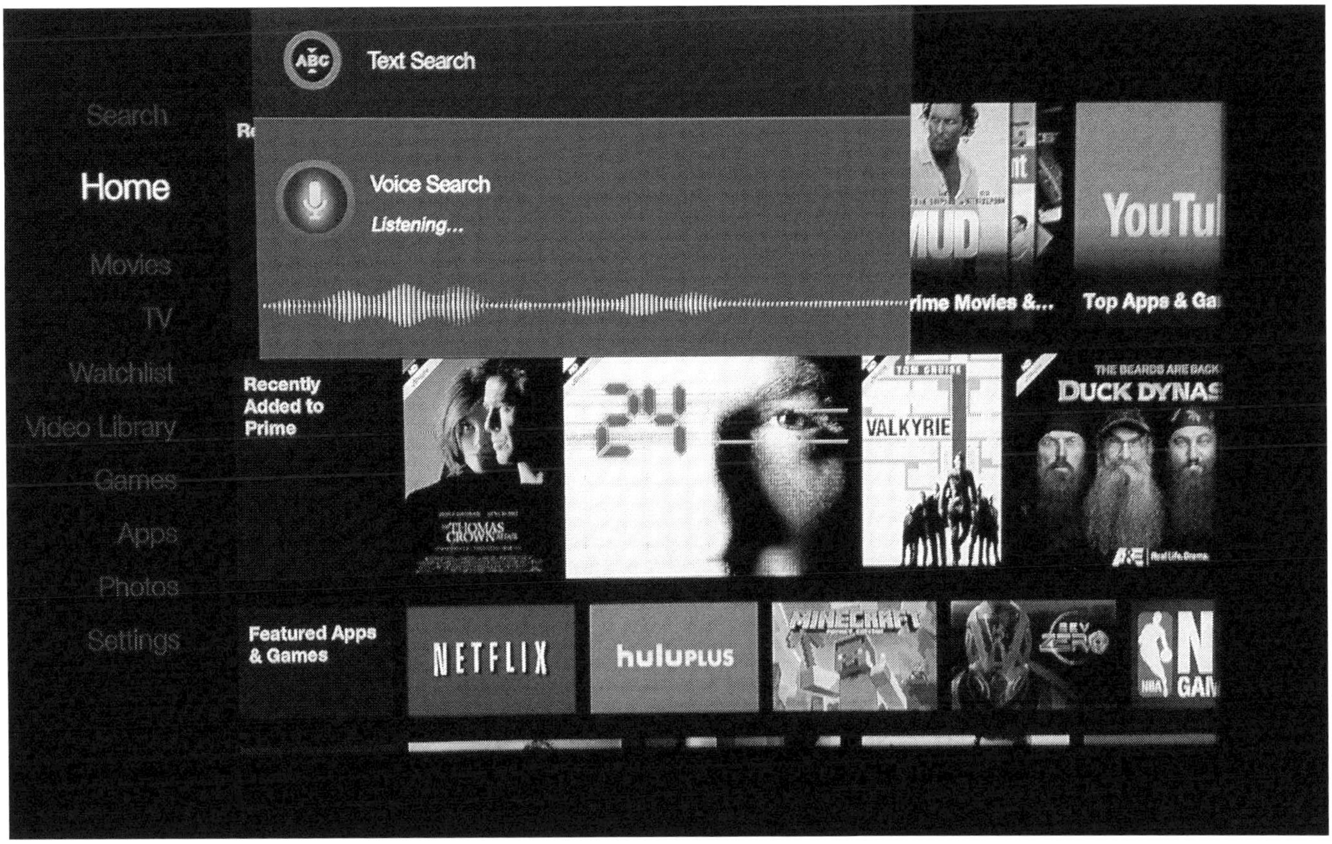

Use the directional trackpad to review your search results, then press the **Select** button to view an item. If your voice search is unsuccessful, press **Up** on the remote control to use an on-screen keyboard for searching.

For best results when using voice search, limit background noise and have only one person speaking at a time.

Access Purchased Movies, TV Shows, Games and Apps

From the **Home** screen, select one of these options from the **Main Menu**:

- **Video Library**: Your purchased or rented Amazon Instant Video movies and TV shows are listed here. (Videos from third-party apps like Netflix and Hulu are accessed directly from the apps, not the Fire TV **Video Library**.)
- **Games**: Your purchased games are listed in **Your Games Library**.
- **Apps**: Your purchased apps are listed in **Your Apps Library**.

Remove Content From the Home Screen

To remove an item from the **Recent** carousel, navigate to the item and select **Remove from Recent**. To remove a title from **Recommended Movies and TV**, navigate to the item and select **Not Interested**.

Change the Screen Saver Settings

From the **Home** screen, select **Settings**, select **System**, then select **Screen Saver**. You may update the screen saver slide style, slide speed, start time, and photo album.

Adjust the Settings

Fire TV will automatically adjust the settings in most cases, but you can use the **Settings** menu to more closely manage your apps, network connection, controllers, screen savers and other items.

From the **Home** screen, select **Settings**:

- **Help**: Access help videos, tips and Amazon customer-service information.
- **My Account**: Register or deregister your Fire TV console. Select **Sync Amazon Content** to make sure your most recent purchases appear on your Fire TV
- **Second Screen**: Allow playback of Amazon videos on nearby compatible tablets. Press the **Select** button on your remote to change the button to **ON**. Disable Second Screen by pressing the **Select** button to change the button to **OFF**.
- **Applications**: Manage your Amazon GameCircle, Appstore and installed application settings. Enable or disable GameCircle nickname sharing, Whispersync for Games, Appstore automatic updates, and in-app purchases. You can also force stop, clear data, clear cache, or uninstall

downloaded applications. (If you clear data, the app won't be deleted but your saved information like game scores may disappear.)

- **Parental Controls**: Block purchases and restrict access to movies, TV shows, games, apps, photos and more. (Fire TV Parental Controls restricts Amazon content only, not third-party apps like Hulu and Netflix.)
- **Controllers**: Pair or update compatible Amazon Fire TV remotes and Bluetooth game controllers.
- **System**: View and manage device information and settings for your Fire TV like screen savers, Wi-Fi network, display calibration, audio and time zone settings.

Set Up Parental Controls

You can block purchases and restrict access to Amazon movies, TV shows, games, apps, photos and more. However, Parental Controls menu doesn't restrict content in third-party applications. These controls are designed by the app provider.

1. From the **Home** screen, select **Settings**, then select **Parental Controls**.
2. Using the remote control, press the **Select** button to turn Parental Controls **On** or **Off**.
3. Enter a Parental Controls PIN, then select **Next**. Your PIN is the same PIN used for other Amazon services, like Instant Video. If you've forgotten your PIN, visit www.amazon.com/PIN to reset it.
4. After you've set a PIN, you can set one or more of the following settings:
    - Require a PIN for all purchases.
    - Require a PIN for Amazon Instant Video only.
    - Block purchasing or viewing of certain content types like games, apps, or photos.
    - Change your Parental Controls PIN.

After enabling Parental Controls, most actions involving content viewing, purchasing or settings changes will require the PIN entry.

3 ► PLAY GAMES AND APPS

First, let's take a look at the Fire TV wireless game controller (sold separately), which can be used to play games and access GameCircle with your FireTV. The game controller can also be used as a remote, providing access to movies, TV shows, games and apps.

To get started using your game controller, install the included two AA batteries and pair the device with your Fire TV. As soon as the batteries are inserted, the controller is "discoverable" by your console. If the game controller isn't discovered, press the **Home** button on the controller for at least five seconds, and then release it.

The game controller isn't compatible with all games. To see which controllers are compatible with a game, navigate to a game, then select **More Info**. On the overview page, you'll see controller information in the **Works With** box. When searching for games and apps, you can also filter the search results by **All**, **Fire TV Remote**, and **Fire TV Game Controller**.

Many third-party Bluetooth game controllers work with Amazon Fire TV. For more information about compatible game controllers, visit www.amazon.com/tv/controllers

Navigating With the Game Controller

- **Back**: Returns you to the previous screen or action.
- **Home**: Returns you to the **Home** screen from any screen on Fire TV.
- **Amazon GameCircle**: Access your GameCircle dashboard while in a game, or access your Games Library.
- **Play, Pause, Rewind, Fast-Forward**: Lets you play, pause, rewind or fast-forward movies and TV shows.
- **Y, X, A, B, left and right shoulder, and trigger buttons**: Mostly used for gaming. Functions can change depending on the game being played.

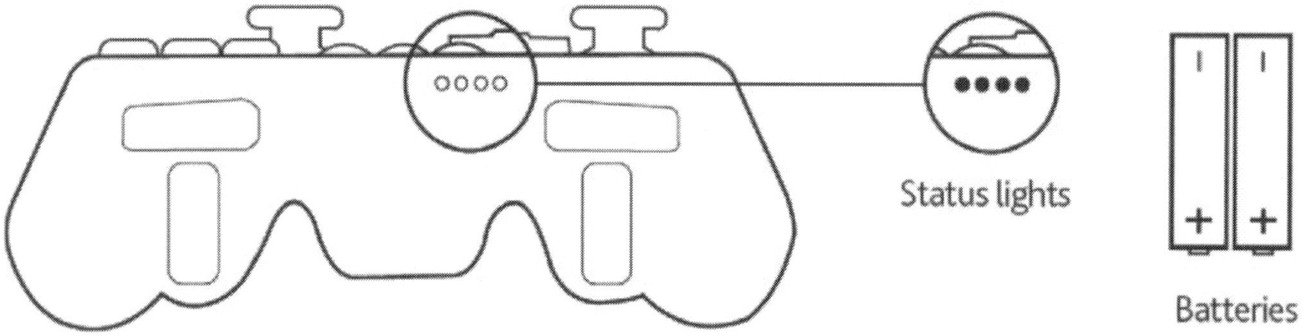

- **Status Lights**: LED indicators at the front of the controller illuminate when the remote is on to indicate which player number the controller has been assigned (when applicable).

Buy and Download Games and Apps

To buy or download games and apps, you must have a 1-Click payment method established with Amazon. To manage those settings, visit www.amazon.com/1click

1. Locate the game or app you want to buy:
   - Browse the categories under **Games** or **Apps**.
   - From the **Home** screen, select **Search** to search for games or apps. Press the **Voice** button on your remote to search using your voice, or press up to use the on-screen keyboard.
2. From your search results, select a game or app to view its overview page. There, you can see which controllers are compatible with the game or app in the **Works With** box. To learn more about compatible game controllers, visit www.amazon.com/tv/controllers
3. Select the **Buy** button, or if the app is free, select the **free** button. You can choose to purchase using your 1-Click payment method or Amazon Coins, if you have them in your account. Once purchased, your game or app begins downloading. When the download is complete, the button changes to **Open**.

Uninstall Games and Apps

You can uninstall games and apps directly from your Fire TV. Games and apps that you purchased and uninstalled can be reinstalled from the game or app overview page.

1. From the **Home** screen, select **Settings**, then select **Applications**.
2. Scroll up or down to find the app you want to uninstall and select it.
3. Select **Uninstall** and then follow the on-screen instructions.

Play Games and Apps

You can play games and apps from your Fire TV. Locate the title in **Your Games Library** or **Your Apps Library**. Select a game or app to begin.

Some games and apps work with the remote control, while other require you to pair the Fire game controller or a compatible game controller. To see which controllers are compatible with a game, navigate to the game and select **More Info**. On the overview page, you'll find the controller information in the **Works With** box. When searching for games and apps, you can also filter the search results by **All**, **Fire TV Remote**, and **Fire TV Game Controller**.

Pairing Additional Remotes and Game Controllers

With Fire TV, you can pair the supplied remote control, Fire TV game controllers, and compatible Bluetooth-enabled third-party controllers. As many as seven can be connected simultaneously.

1. From the **Home** screen, select **Settings**, and then select **Controllers**.

2. Select **Amazon Fire TV Remotes** (or for game controllers, select **Bluetooth Gamepads**), and then select **Add New Remote** (or **Add Bluetooth Gamepads**).
3. Press and hold the **Home** button on your remote for five seconds. After the remote or game controller is discovered, select it from the list of discovered devices using your already-paired, existing remote or game controller.

4 ► ADVANCED TIPS AND TRICKS

Use Fire TV as a Display Mirroring Destination

You can use your Fire TV to wirelessly relay your Kindle Fire HDX screen and audio to your TV screen. Before you begin, ensure your Fire TV and Kindle Fire HDX are turned on and connected to the same wireless network.

To begin Display Mirroring from your Kindle Fire HDX to your TV:

1. On your Kindle Fire HDX, swipe down from the top of the screen to open **Quick Settings**, and then tap **Settings**.
2. Tap **Display & Sounds**, and then tap **Display Mirroring**. Your Fire TV device should appear in the list of **Devices**.
3. Select your Fire TV device. It may take 10 to 20 seconds for your Kindle Fire screen to appear on your TV screen. To stop mirroring your Kindle Fire, tap **Stop Mirroring**.

Use Fire TV With a Second Screen Device

You can enhance your viewing experience by using “Second Screen” features from compatible devices like your Kindle Fire HDX. This lets you use your Kindle Fire to control the playback of an Amazon video on your TV. While you watch the video on your HDTV, you can use the X-Ray feature on your Kindle Fire to view trivia about the actors and music for each scene.

To begin, ensure that your tablet and Fire TV are turned on and connected to the Internet, and both devices are registered to the same Amazon account. For best results, ensure both devices are connected to the same network.

To use Second Screen from your tablet:

1. Find an Amazon Instant Video movie or TV show you’d like to watch. The **Watch** button should have the **Send To** icon enabled on it.
2. Select the **Send To** icon, then select your Amazon Fire TV from the list.
3. The video begins playing on your TV. While watching, you can control playback by tapping your Kindle Fire’s **Play**, **Pause**, **Jump Back** or video **progress bar**. Your tablet will also display related X-Ray information when available.

To use Second Screen when you already have content playing on your TV:

1. Swipe down from the top of your tablet to display the notification screen. You should see a notification for the content currently being played.
2. Select the **Play/Pause** button on the notification to pause or resume the video.
3. Select the notification row to control the video playback with the media controls or launch the synchronized X-Ray experience, when available.

Turn On or Customize Closed Captions

While browsing Amazon Instant Video movies and TV shows, videos that include closed captions appear with the closed caption symbol, "CC," on their overview pages. Most videos that support closed captions include English text, although other languages are sometimes available too.

To watch a video with closed captions:

1. Play the video of your choice.
2. After playback has started, press the **Menu** button on the Fire TV remote and select **Turn Captions On**.
   - After you turn on captions, navigate left or right with the trackpad on the remote control to select the font size and color scheme for the caption text. Your selections apply to all videos you view until you change your selections again.
3. Press the **Menu** button again to return to view playback with captions on.

To turn captions off, press the **Menu** button on the remote and select **Turn Captions Off**.

You can also manage your Instant Video closed caption settings at www.amazon.com/cc under **Subtitle Preference**. To update how closed caption text appears when you watch Netflix, visit www.netflix.com/youraccount and select **Subtitle Appearance.** You may also be able to update how closed caption text appears with other video applications on Fire TV.

View Photos and Personal Videos

Your Amazon Cloud Drive photos and personal videos are available on your Fire TV. To add photos to your Cloud Drive account from a mobile device or desktop computer, you need to install the Cloud Drive app or you can add photos through your web browser. For more information, navigate to your Fire TV's **Photos** from the **Home** screen, then select **Add Photos & Videos**.

1. From the **Home** screen, select **Photos**, then press right or left on the remote to browse your photos and videos.
2. Press the **Select** button to view a single photo or play a personal video.

You can disable access to your photos and personal videos by setting up Parental Controls.

View Slideshows

You can launch full-screen slideshows of your photos on your TV.

1. From the **Home** screen, select **Photos** to view your photo albums.
2. Select a photo album, then select **Start Slideshow**.
   - The album slideshow automatically advances through photos located in the current album or list you're viewing.
   - The slideshow automatically restarts when it reaches the end.
   - Press left or right to advance or go back in the album at your desired speed.

Set Screen Savers

You can customize your Amazon Fire TV screen saver by selecting a photo or album from Amazon Cloud Drive.

To add photos to your Cloud Drive account from a mobile device or computer, you need to install the Cloud Drive app or add photos through your web browser. For more information, visit **Photos** from the **Home** screen of your Fire TV, then select **Add Photos & Videos**.

1. From the **Home** screen, select **Photos** to view your photo albums.
2. Select a photo or album, then select **Set As Screen Saver**. The screen saver will launch when your Fire TV is left idle.

To manage screen saver settings such as the slide style, slide speed, and start time, press the **Home** button, select **Settings**, select **System**, and then select **Screen Saver**.

Turn off In-App Purchasing

You can prevent accidental in-app purchases by turning on Parental Controls. When purchasing is enabled, you can purchase items such as in-game currency or premium unlocks within an app. If you don't want in-app purchases to occur, disable the option:

1. From the **Home** screen, select **Settings**, then select **Parental Controls**. (If you've forgotten your PIN, visit www.amazon.com/PIN)
2. Press the **Select** button again to change the button to **ON**.
3. Enter your Amazon Parental Controls PIN (if you already have one) or create a new PIN and select **Next**. Parental Controls options will appear.
4. Select **PIN Protect Purchases** to change the button to **ON**.

Understanding GameCircle

Amazon GameCircle enhances your gaming experience by storing your achievements, high scores, and time played in the Cloud, enabling you to compare with your friends and others. For games and apps that use Whispersync for Games, GameCircle syncs your game progress across all your Fire devices.

When you open a GameCircle-enabled game, a Welcome Back message appears. To see more information, press the Home button on your remote or press the GameCircle button on your Amazon Fire game controller.

Hide your GameCircle Profile

If you wish, you can hide your gaming information from the GameCircle Settings screen. While your profile is hidden, you won't be able to send or receive friend requests or view other users' profiles.

1. From the **Home** screen, select **Settings**, then select **Applications**, then select **Amazon GameCircle**.
2. Select **Share your GameCircle Nickname** so the feature is turned **Off**.

5 ▶ RECOMMENDED APPS FOR FIRE TV

Locate these apps by searching for them in the Amazon AppStore and having them sent to your Fire TV. The great thing about apps is that new ones arrive frequently, and existing apps are continuously updated and improved.

Above: The app store page for Netflix, the leading streaming-video service for movies and television

No doubt one of the most popular apps for Fire TV is Netflix, which has been the king of streaming video for several years. The company was started in 1997 as a DVD-by-mail rental company, and it still operates the DVD rental business.

Netflix

At this writing, Netflix charges $7.99 a month for unlimited movies and TV episodes. There are no commercials, and you can pause, rewind, fast-forward and rewatch as often as you wish. Netflix offers a free one-month trial membership and with a membership, family members can sign into your account at the same time and watch different things. The service has parental controls, so if you have young children in the home, you can prevent them from accessing adult content.

The typical Hollywood movie that was in theaters a few months ago probably isn't available through Netflix's streaming-video service, but is available in through the Netflix DVD-by-mail program.

And one more point: If you subscribe to a metered Internet service, such as one from a satellite provider, or subscribe to a basic Internet speed package, you might still want to watch Netflix's DVDs.

The breadth of content available through Netflix has encouraged many consumers to "cut the cord" and abandon their traditional cable-TV service—thereby avoiding the inevitable yearly price increases—not to mention the cable company's insistence on charging subscribers for hundreds of channels they don't want. On the other hand, many households see value in each of the services, and in many cases, they maintain subscriptions to Netflix and cable-TV packages.

Comparing Amazon Prime Video to Netflix

Until Fire TV, one of Netflix's big advantages over Amazon Prime Video was the ease with which customers could access Netflix streaming-video through a wide variety of game consoles, apps for smartphones and tablets, and set-top boxes. Newer Samsung TVs have a Netflix button on the remote control, which instantly launches the Netflix service. By contrast, Amazon's Prime Video has traditionally been available only to users of its Kindle Fire tablets and desktop computer users, leaving others without very many easy ways to view Amazon video on a TV—the main exception being the Sony Playstation game console. Fire TV has obliterated that main stumbling block for customers who want to watch Amazon video on their TVs.

Although Amazon Prime Video and Netflix offer much of the same content, the pricing is vastly different. First, let's take a look at the pricing for Netflix and Amazon. At this writing, Netflix charges $7.99 a month for unlimited movies and TV episodes streamed to your TV, computer, or handheld device. Meanwhile, Amazon costs $99 per year, which works out to $8.25 per month. With both services, there are no commercials, and you can pause, rewind, fast-forward and rewatch as often as you wish. Each offers a free one-month trial membership. Each offers parental controls, so if you have young children in the home, you can prevent them from accessing adult content.

One major difference with Netflix is its DVD-by-mail service, which starts at an additional $7.99 per month. (The $7.99 entitles you to rent one DVD at a time, and for additional fees, you can have two or more DVDs rented at the same time—which is handy in case you want to have a double-feature night at your home theater.)

If you've never considered Netflix before, you might be wondering: Why should I care about its DVD rental service if I already have streaming video? After all, with the streaming video, you don't have to wait for a DVD to come in the mail; you simply choose a video and begin watching. The answer: Netflix's DVD selection is much, much larger than its streaming service. Many movie studios don't give permission for streaming access to their content, or in other cases, the cost is prohibitive for Netflix to include the movie in their regular streaming service. On the other hand, virtually every film made in recent decades is available through Netflix's DVD service, which dwarfs Amazon's selection.

Here's an example to illustrate how Netflix differs from Amazon: The typical Hollywood movie that was in theaters a few months ago probably isn't available through Netflix's streaming-video service, but is available in through the Netflix DVD-by-mail program. Meanwhile, the same movie is often available through Amazon's streaming-video service, but it will cost you extra—perhaps $5 to $15 for a 24-hour "rental." Another choice is to "buy" it from Amazon for unlimited watching at a cost of perhaps $15 to $20. The exact prices depend on what sort of deal Amazon was able to work out with the movie studio—and how much we consumers are willing to pay for the pleasure of viewing it.

Another typical example: A recent TV series might be available through Amazon at $1.99 per episode, while it's free through Netflix's streaming service. On the other hand, Amazon has been very busy adding new video content, and over time, it's possible that Amazon will pull even with Netflix in terms of selection.

One additional consideration for video buffs: In many cases, the quality of video available on Blu-Ray DVDs exceeds that of streaming video offered by Netflix or Amazon. Meanwhile, Amazon's web site offers great deals on individual and boxed-sets of DVDs, and true bargain-hunters can sometimes find used DVDs for sale on Amazon for pennies on the dollar. But the bottom line is, when you consider the convenience of streaming video and the benefits for consumers who partake in Amazon's shipping discounts, plus its digital entertainment offerings, Amazon Prime becomes more irresistable by the day.

Crackle – Movies & TV CRACKLE IT'S ON

Crackle might be called the "poor man's Netflix." The selection of content is sparse compared to Netflix, but the service is free. In exchange for enjoying the free videos, you must endure regular interruptions for commercials, similar to broadcast television.

Crackle has some original content, too, such as the new Jerry Seinfield show *Comedians in Cars Getting Coffee*. You can also view familiar TV shows like *Seinfeld*, *The Shield*, and *Damages*.

Red Bull TV

This free service specializes in "extreme" sports, including bike, skateboarding, motorsports, snowboarding, surfing, aircraft racing, paragliding, adventure and music. Some of the videos are live, some are prerecorded. (The name "Red Bull" originates from the energy drink company that sponsors the channel.)

You can choose to view an hour-long rolling block of clips from all sorts of playgrounds—surf, snow, break dancing and more—that's refreshed daily.

Red Bull TV suggests that their videos are exclusive, although some of them are apparently available elsewhere. In any case, Red Bull TV does a fine job of collecting extreme sports videos and weeding out the junk, an experience you seldom find on YouTube, for example.

Pandora PANDORA

Pandora is a personalized online radio service. You can stream your favorite music instantly by telling Pandora what songs, performers or genres you enjoy, and Pandora delivers more of the music it determines you'll enjoy based on input from you and other subscribers who listen to similar music. Pandora allows you to create up to 100 personalized stations.

Pandora serves up nearly a century of popular recordings—old and new, well known and wholly obscure—to deliver a listening experience you'll enjoy. For each track, you can provide a thumbs-up or thumbs-down rating to encourage Pandora to play similar music (or not). The service includes a wide array of comedy recordings, too.

Pandora has a free and a paid service. The free service includes advertising, and for a subscription fee of $3.99 a month, you can eliminate the advertising. The paid version of Pandora also offers a higher audio quality, although you might be hard-pressed to hear the difference, depending on what type of equipment you're using to play the service.

Hulu Plus huluPLUS

Hulu allows you to watch streaming TV shows for $7.99 per month. The company offers a free one-week trial.

With limited advertising, Hulu Plus offers all current season episodes of popular shows like *Glee*, *Family Guy*, and *Modern Family*, and full series runs (all episodes from every season) of popular library shows, including *The X-Files*, *Arrested Development*, *Desperate Housewives*, *Battlestar Galactica*, *Monk*, *Saturday Night Live*, *Law & Order: Special Victims Unit*, *Ugly Betty*, *Buffy the Vampire Slayer*, and more.

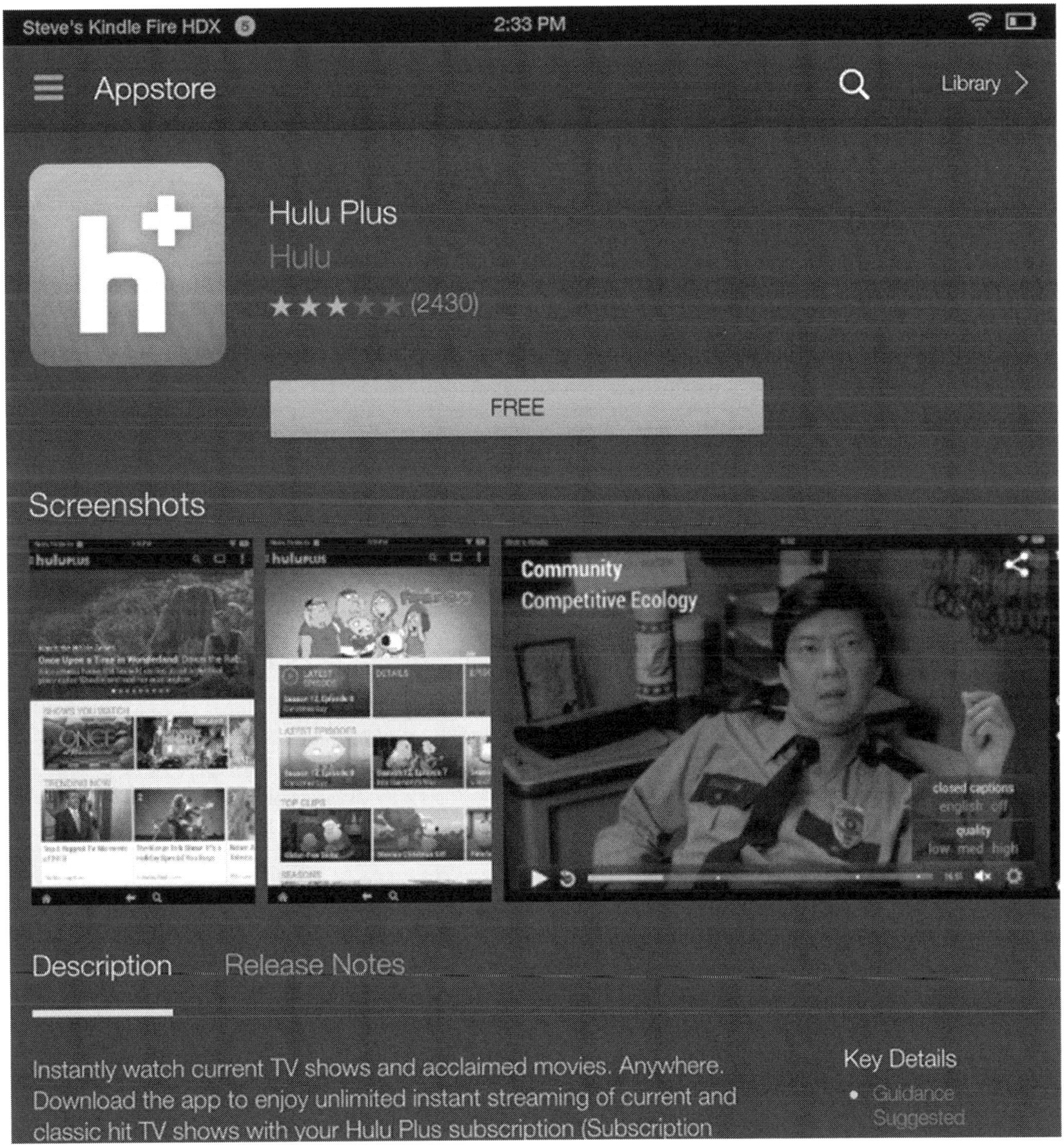

The AppStore listing for Hulu Plus

Hulu struggles in a comparison to Netflix for several reasons. Although the subscription fees are similar, Hulu offers a narrower selection of content, plus the service shows advertisements. Netflix has no ads.

Vevo

Vevo offers music videos and some original, live music programming. Its music catalog includes 75,000 videos from more than 21,000 artists, and it provides a somewhat better experience than using YouTube to watch music videos. For example, if you search for a certain artist or song, you'll quickly find the official video without having to wade through knockoff videos submitted by amateurs. Creating an account isn't necessary, but it does enable a more personalized experience. You can easily share your favorites via Facebook and Twitter. This free service is supported by advertising, which appears before some of the videos you select.

Plex

Plex is a media server that enables you to play your personal videos on your TV. If you have a large collection of video files stored on your computer, Plex can come in very handy. It can handle virtually any format of video file and stream it to your Fire TV.

Watch ESPN

The WatchESPN app lets you watch the best of ESPN on your Fire TV, including live games and studio shows with 24/7 access to ESPN, ESPN2, ESPN3, ESPNU, ESPNews and ESPN Deportes. You can also watch on-demand clips of the latest news and highlights.

Events include: Monday Night Football, NBA Regular Season and Playoffs, Major League Baseball, The Masters, U.S. Open and The Open Championship, College Football and Basketball, and all four Grand Slam tennis events.

This app also provides up-to-the-minute news, highlights and analysis with live streaming of your favorite ESPN shows, including: SportsCenter, PTI, College GameDay, Mike & Mike, SportsNation, and Baseball Tonight.

Although the app is free, you'll need to be an ESPN subscriber; access is governed by your cable and Internet service provider. The first time you access video through Watch ESPN, you'll log in with your cable TV user name and password. Participating providers include AT&T U-verse, Bright House Networks, Comcast XFINITY, Cox, Dish Network, Google Fiber, Midcontinent Communications, Optimum, Time Warner Cable and Verizon FiOS TV.

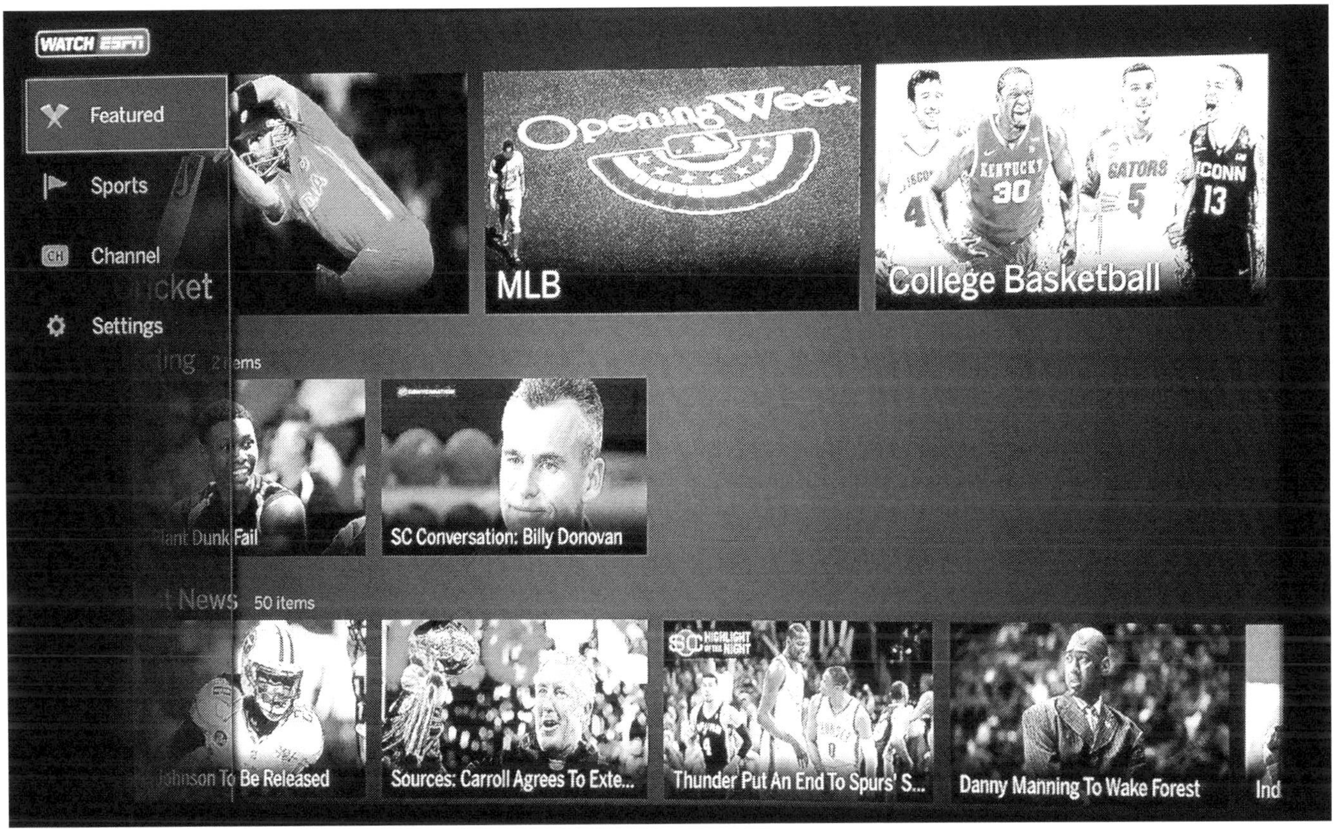

Above: It's sports 24/7 on Watch ESPN.

Showtime Anytime

Watch Showtime with your existing subscription through participating cable companies. You get unlimited on-demand access to full seasons of original series, movies, sports, comedy and more. Shows include *Homeland*, *Masters of Sex*, *Ray Donovan*, *Shameless*, *Dexter*, *House of Lies*, *Californication* and more.

HuffPost Live

HuffPost Live is a live-streaming video network that lets you be part of the conversation. This app uses the most engaging stories on The Huffington Post news website as the jumping-off point for real-time conversations and commentary—and invites viewers to join the discussion as on-air guests. Topics range from current events and entertainment to tech, parenting,health and fitness.

iHeartRadio

Listen to your favorite live radio stations or create your own. This streaming radio app lets you enjoy free music, news, talk, sports and commercial-free custom stations. Select from thousands of real radio stations playing pop, country, hip-hop, R&B, rock, talk, news, sports and more.

Vimeo

Watch videos from the world's best creators on your TV. View staff picks, browse your feed, and add videos to your Watch Later queue. Includes short films from independent and student filmmakers. Some of the videos cost money, but the vast majority are free.

Bloomberg TV

Bloomberg TV, a live, 24-hour global business and financial news channel, offers an extensive collection of videos covering the biggest and most important stories in the business world. The videos in Bloomberg TV are well organized for easy discovery and include key segments from Bloomberg TV's critically acclaimed shows like *Bloomberg West*, *Brink* and *Charlie Rose* as well as topics such as technology, autos, luxury and travel.

TuneIn Radio

Another streaming radio app, TuneIn boasts 100,000 stations and 2 million on-demand programs. Add stations, songs and shows to your Favorites, browse and listen to over 100,000 stations of sports, news, weather, talk, podcasts, music and national networks like BBC, NPR, TEDTalks and more. Create custom music stations featuring songs from the artist you select and similar music using their catalog of more than 16 million songs.

DailyBurn

This app provides HD-quality workout videos, programmed for 10 minutes to an hour. It includes everything from bodyweight training and kettlebells to dance and yoga—so you will always get the perfect workout.

YouTube

Search, browse and play thousands of videos. This app is a bookmark that provides a direct link to YouTube's TV-optimized website. The app performs very well for the Fire TV but searching for videos is a bit awkward.

AOL On

Watch the latest videos—from top news stories and entertainment from Reuters, Entertainment Tonight, Martha Stewart, and many more sources. AOL On provides breaking news, a quick laugh, the newest tech demo, or an easy recipe for dinner.

Flixter

Keeps you up-to-date on the latest theater and DVD movie releases and reviews. Browse box office favorites and new releases, view show times, and order tickets. If you're a Netflix subscriber, you can log in directly from this app to add movies to—or remove movies from—your Netflix queue.

Qello

Streams a wide selection of high-quality concert films and music documentaries. Access premium and curated content, design your own setlists, view live Q&A sessions with artists, see monthly reviews from tastemakers, and more.

Also provides archival concerts, including many rare and digitally re-mastered classic concerts from Ike and Tina and the Beatles to Jimmy Hendrix, Elvis and Bob Dylan.

Frequency

Frequency gives you a single place to watch internet video on your TV from sources all across the web, including YouTube. Instead of going to all your favorite websites, social networks, blogs and apps to watch video, Frequency finds and organizes the newest videos into streaming channels—just like TV. The award-winning interface turns internet video into continuously playing channels that you select.

Bob the Trader

Bob The Trader lets you follow Tom Sosnoff, the stock, futures, and options trading guru, as he trades every day during market hours. Get real-time notifications directly on your Kindle Fire device each time Tom makes a trade, and stream his live show Monday through Friday on the tastytrade network as he talks about options strategies and trading the market.

Minecraft

Minecraft is a wildly popular video game enjoyed by children and adults. The game involves placing blocks to build things and going on adventures. Pocket Edition includes Survival and Creative modes, multiplayer over a local Wi-Fi network, and randomly generated worlds. You can craft, create and breed anywhere in the world so long as you have hands to spare and time to burn.

Riptide GP2

This game features rocket-powered hydro jets racing around futuristic tracks across a dynamic and interactive water surface. Includes intense water racing action, upgradeable hydro jets and riders, improved graphics, an all-new career mode, and a whole new stunt system with dozens of new tricks.

Asphalt 8: Airborne

This is an arcade-style racing game. Perform dynamic, high-speed aerial stunts in an intense driving experience powered by a brand-new physics engine here.

Okay, we've skimmed the cream of the crop, but we've barely scratched the surface. For the complete, up-to-the-minute listing of Fire TV apps, visit http://www.amazon.com/b?ie=UTF8&node=7031433011. And check there often because new apps are always being introduced and added.

6 ▶ TROUBLESHOOTING COMMON PROBLEMS

Can't Connect to Wi-Fi

If you can't connect to a Wi-Fi network from Fire TV, check that your wireless connection is turned on.

Check this first:

- Make sure you connect Fire TV to one of these network or router types:
  - Open, WEP, WPA/WPA2 PSK, and WPA/WPA2 EAP encrypted networks
  - B, G, and N routers on 2.4Ghz
  - A and N routers on 5Ghz
  - Hidden networks
- Make sure wireless connectivity is enabled on Fire TV. From the **Home** screen, select **Settings**, select **System**, then select **Wi-Fi**.
- Make sure you know your network password, if required. If you see a lock icon, a password is required. (This password is not your Amazon password.)
- Make sure your Internet connection is working. Restarting your router and modem will resolve most Wi-Fi issues.
- Don't enclose Fire TV in a cabinet as this may reduce signal strength.

If all else fails, unplug the power cord from your Fire TV for three seconds, then plug the power cord back in.

Can't Pair a Remote Control or Game Controller

If you can't pair your Fire TV remote control or wireless game controller, it might not be within range or compatible.

Check this first:

- Amazon Fire TV is compatible with Fire TV remotes, Fire game controllers, and many third-party Bluetooth-enabled game controllers. For more information, visit www.amazon.com/tv/controllers
- Don't place Fire TV in a cabinet as this reduces signal strength.

- Your remote must be within 30 feet of Fire TV.
- Re-install the batteries. You have five minutes to pair your remote with Fire TV before it re-enters sleep mode.
- If your remote isn't discovered, press the **Home** button for five to 10 seconds.

Or disconnect the power cord from your Fire TV for three seconds, then plug the power cord back in.

Basic Troubleshooting for Fire TV

For issues like a frozen screen, app errors, or problems with content like movies, TV shows, games and apps, try these steps:

Problems purchasing or accessing content:

- Confirm that Fire TV is connected to the Internet. A connection is required to buy, stream, and sync your content.
- Verify that you're connected to the Internet by visiting **Home**, select **Settings**, **System**, then **Wi-Fi**.
- Verify that your 1-Click payment method is set up correctly. Visit www.amazon.com/1click

Movies, photos or purchased content not showing:

- Verify that Fire TV is registered to the correct Amazon account.
- To verify your registration, go to the **Home** screen, select **Settings**, then select **My Account**. If you see the wrong account listed, select the account, then select **Deregister**. Select **Register** to associate the correct account.

Specific app issues:

- From the **Home** screen, select **Settings**, then select **Applications**. Select the application you want to modify . Now you can change settings, clear data, clear cache, force stop, or uninstall the application if you're still experiencing problems.

Remote not connecting:

- Before trying to re-pair your remote, first check that it has a fresh set of AAA batteries.
- Try unplugging the power cord from your Fire TV and then plugging it back in.

Forgot Amazon Instant Video PIN:

Visit www.amazon.com/PIN

- In the **Your Amazon Instant Video PIN** section, type a 5-digit number to set up your PIN, or click **View/Edit Your PIN** to change your current PIN.

Index